# 101
# Inspirations
# from the
# Heart

# 101

# INSPIRATIONS

## *From the* Heart

## June Elaine Bondy

O'LEARY
PUBLISHING
*The Influencers Press*

**Bonita Springs, FL**

Published in the United States by O'Leary Publishing
www.olearypublishing.com

For bulk group pricing please email:
info@olearypublishing.com

The views, information, or opinions expressed in this book are solely those of the authors involved and do not necessarily represent those of O'Leary Publishing, LLC.

ISBN-13: 978-1-7337104-6-6 (Print)
ISBN-13: 978-1-7337104-7-3 (e-Book)

Cover Design by Christine Dupre
Photography by Julie Renner
Interior Design by Douglas Williams
Editing by Sharman Monroe
Proofreading by Hillary Sigale

Library of Congress Control Number: 2019910250

Printed in the United States of America

# ADVANCE PRAISE

*"So easy to understand. I reread your articles frequently and try to apply them. Thank you!"*
**— Tamara**

*"Great site. Really appreciate your thoughts and advice."*
**— Sonia**

*"Enjoying your wise sayings. Making life clearer for real life is not easy."*
**— Kalie (Jamaica)**

*"Good to read. Nice from the heart and soul."*
**— Saalam**

*"So helpful with relationships and home balancing and just life as it is."*
**— Amy**

*"Very good to learn from you."*
**— Tasha (Moscow)**

*"So nice to hear and learn. There are many troubles these days. You have helped me so much."*
**— Peppi**

*"Interesting. Informative. With feeling. Nice to learn and not feel alone."*
**— Kali**

*"We like to read and talk about your thoughts. Kansas says 'Hi'."*
**— Kayla**

*This book is written to inspire the person
who has faced adversity and may not know
where to turn or what to do next.*

# CONTENTS

# Acknowledgments

This book would not be possible without the inspiration and support of Robert. He has been my rock and my cheerleader. I love you.

I would also like to thank my children. They have always been there for me in hard times and in good times. I love you all.

# INTRODUCTION

June Elaine was born in the Midwest of the United States on a farm. Later, she moved to the south and enjoys the sun-filled days and evening sunsets. She has survived many challenging life events, but has always managed to come out on top.

She began writing at the age of 73 and launched her popular blog June Elaine's Nuggets, www.juneelainesnuggets.com, which has been viewed by people all over the world. This book was inspired by the website. She hopes that *101 Inspirations from the Heart* will encourage you to *be the best you can be* and to know that it is never too late to fulfill your dreams and enjoy your life. Never stop dreaming.

# 1

WEEDS IN MY
GARDEN

Do you have weeds in your garden? My own personal space, my garden, has had many weeds over the years. They often became domineering, influential, bossy, and very controlling, and tried to choke out some of the more beautiful plants that were trying their best to grow.

How did I break free? It took a close death in my family to make me realize that I did have a fruitful mind and thoughts that were worth sharing.

Over the years, I had become too submissive to the controlling power of my weeds. It was easier to agree and stay quiet than to stand up for myself and my thoughts. Even though I thought my agenda was worth hearing, I stayed inside myself.

Were my ideas worth hearing? Yes, they were. Was my self-worth worth exploring? Yes, it was. Inside I knew I was a good person. It just had to be brought out. God and a very good friend helped me to achieve my mental freedom and restore my confidence. It is wonderful to be able to express myself and know that what I say is worth hearing. It is wonderful to talk and be respected.

This new-found freedom was in me all along. I just had to have the confidence to trust God and to follow wonderful advice that encouraged me, instead of crushing me. Today my garden is slowly being restored to its natural beauty. It's never too late to weed your garden.

> *"The hardest prison to escape is in your mind. Free yourself."* **— Unknown**

# 2

❦

# HANDLING
# REJECTION

Rejection comes in many forms. As a child, I felt rejected because love was not expressed in my family. I didn't feel close to any family members because of it. As an adult, I have also felt rejected. Admittedly, some of that was my fault. Because of this persistent rejection, I habitually put myself down and did not respect my own opinions or self-worth.

Now, as a senior citizen, I know I am a child of God and that I matter as much as anyone else. I am proud of the fact that I am my own person. No one can take that away from me.

You can become your own person too. Don't let rejection keep you stuck in the same place for a lifetime. Don't wait for a tragic incident to make you realize who you are. You are a child of God.

Have you waited too long to be who you want to be?

> *"Be yourself, everyone else is taken."* — **Oscar Wilde**

# 3

## Why Am I Here On This Earth?

I hope that my life here on earth has made an impact on someone. I've not set out to change someone's life, but maybe I have influenced or encouraged someone in their journey. My life hasn't been easy, but I have tried to keep my eyes on God and do what He wanted me to do.

Do I ever get angry? Of course. Do I ever do what I want to do instead of listening to God? The answer is yes. It is hard to always do the right thing. The devil makes his appearance and tries to get us to do what he wants.

But, if we just listen to the quiet voice of God, we can determine what is right from what is wrong and we will know what to do in difficult situations.

> *"Listen in silence, because if your heart is full of other things, you cannot hear the voice of God."* **—Mother Teresa**

*4*

## DON'T EVER
## GIVE UP

Hopefully, depression will not be a persistent part of a person's life. But sometimes it is unavoidable. It may be brought on through no fault of our own. Sometimes depression is a medical issue, and sometimes it is perpetuated by the people around us.

Oftentimes, wrong decisions are made and we feel like we have to live with them, whether it is for a religious reason or just because of a situation that we feel we are trapped in.

I was in the autumn of my life when I finally had the chance to break free from my old feelings and decisions and I was finally able to live. I met someone special who encouraged me, saw the potential in me, and loved me for me. What a feeling of life, and freedom, and pure enjoyment!

I may not have that many years left in this life, but the years will be full of hope and contentment. The next life will be even better. I am practicing for the next life by fully enjoying this life.

Smile at someone else for no reason. It may be the only smile that they receive that day. Help someone, for they may not know how to ask. Doing this will only make you a happier and better person. Never give up hope, for yourself or for someone else.

*"Stars can't shine without darkness."* **—Unknown**

# 5

LIFE IS
LIKE WATER

L ife is like water. We experience ripples and waves. A little ripple is over in a short time, but sometimes a wave can grow fiercer and stronger as the days go on. We don't always know how to handle or endure a wave. A wave might be caused by a spouse or a child or even a "friend."

We worry and lose sleep. Sometimes talking about your wave is not welcomed or even listened to, and it is certainly not accepted. I have thrown weird words into a conversation and the person that I was talking to didn't even realize. Why? Because they were not listening, nor did they care.

How can we handle this? Busy oneself with something else. Why waste your breath? We can ride this wave even though, at times, we may feel like we are drowning. The tide will change and this too shall pass.

> *"One of the most sincere forms of respect*
> *is actually listening to what another*
> *has to say."* — **Bryant H. McGill**

# 6

## WE ARE
## ALL GIFTS

We are all gifts to ourselves and to others. We just have to be unwrapped. Layer by layer, we become the person that we are meant to be. We may not see it at first, but we are all unique and great. We must look inside ourselves before we can truly know who we are.

I was beaten down, emotionally, for most of my life. It took the loss of a close family member for me to realize that I was a strong and valuable person and that I should be heard. First, I had to work on myself. I had to learn to like myself. I made decisions, and, whether they were right or wrong, I stuck to them. I made myself talk to a stranger, even if it was just to say hello. I went out to eat with friends even though I would have rather stayed home. My home was my cocoon. Like a butterfly, I had to free myself.

This isn't easy. Don't let anyone tell you differently. It takes time. You have to take baby steps, but finally, you will be walking and maybe even running with confidence.

This is all done with God at your side. Remember the poem Footsteps in the Sand? You may only see one set of footprints—that means God is carrying you. You may see two sets of footprints—God is walking beside you. Day-by-day, you will practice and finally succeed in becoming a confident person. Not only will you like yourself, but other people will also like you and respect you.

> *"Nobody can make you happy until you're happy with yourself first."* **— Unknown**

# 7

## CHILDREN

Do you remember when your children were young and you dreamed of their future? You thought of when they would become adults and be successful on their own. You and your spouse could finally have time to yourselves and you could do things that you had only dreamed of for years. It seemed so attainable at the time. Your daughter would be a doctor and your son, even though he didn't like school, would be working in some kind of trade and be happy.

You didn't see the hiccups along the way. The course of their lives and yours changed in ways you had never dreamed of. Marriages, relationships, and sickness crept in and changed everything. You still loved them but had to accept and deal with their decisions. Could you have changed the outcome? Maybe, but you taught them to think for themselves and to make their own decisions. You had to put their lives in God's hands and pray that they would be guided in the right direction. As they grew up and time spun on, faster and faster, you came to appreciate them, and the life that you and your children had made, even more.

Nothing is perfect. Life throws us curve balls. We have to go with these curves and learn the lessons that we are being taught. A wise person once told me, "We have to play the hand that we are dealt."

I am older now and have spent time reflecting on the past. Would I have done things differently? Of course, but I made the best decisions that I knew how to make at the time. No child comes with a manual. No marriage comes with a manual. We just do our best.

*"It is not what you do for your children, but what you have taught them to do for themselves, that will make them successful human beings."* **—Ann Landers**

# 8

# DONUTS

Have you ever looked at and studied a donut? Yes, it is tempting and oh so yummy looking. It also has a hole.

This is sometimes how life is. We see a new relationship as tempting and yummy, but somewhere there is a hole. We don't see the "hole" until after we are married and perhaps have brought children into the relationship.

The "hole" could be hiding in a fun personality or in a connection to relatives. We are working so hard to keep everything perfect for our children that we ignore the signs happening around us.

We might even look at this donut and think that it is drying up, or getting stale or, worse, moldy. Now what do we do? Some of us keep trying to stop the donut from getting too stale and falling apart. Sometimes it is better to throw the donut away and maybe start over, but where does that leave the children and what does this teach them?

Some people put their own feelings first. This may be acceptable, as we do tend to lose ourselves. We have to dig deep and locate the person that we used to be. It may take some experiences and heartaches to get to where we want to be, but we can do it.

Some people put their children first, but should we continue to satisfy their needs and forget our own?

My children are adults now with children of their own. It's understandable that they have their own lives and you want that for them. But don't forget about you. Make peace with yourself. You did your best. God sees that. If you have a chance, grab that golden ring.

*"No matter what your age, there is life worth living."* — **Unknown**

# 9

## CREATE YOUR
## OWN HOLIDAYS

Holidays can be joyful, but also sad. If you were raised in a home that was festive and you had family nearby to celebrate with, you were excited and happy for the holidays.

If you were raised in a home that was poor and could not celebrate, you probably dread the holidays coming up.

The point that I want to make is that you can "create" your holiday the way you want to and you can "celebrate" it the way that you want. Create your own traditions and make your own memories. It's not about gifts; it's about being together and celebrating with each other.

Enjoy the time that you have with family. It can be taken away, forever, in a split second.

*"Celebrate the happiness that friends are always giving. Make every day a holiday and celebrate just living."* **— Amanda Bradley**

# 10

# WHAT A PRIVILEGE

What an unexpected privilege I have had. My older grandchildren lived about 1300 miles away from me while they were growing up. I did not get to see them very often, even though we stayed close. They have since moved to my area and it is wonderful to have them near.

The real surprise came when my first child had a child of his own when he was in his forties. I was able to watch her sometimes while she was a baby. I got to watch her roll over for the first time. I was there when she took her first steps.

She is now in school and I still get to watch her for a day every now and then. Just being able to witness her imagination and her huge vocabulary, even her growing knowledge of letters, words, and numbers, has been a privilege.

I most likely will not live long enough to see her married or have children, but I have the privilege of being with her now. I can go to her recitals and enjoy Grandparent's Day and see her classroom activities. I will savor these moments knowing that the bond we form now will stay in her memory forever. She will always remember her Nana.

*"Simply enjoy life and the great pleasures that come with it."* — **Karolina Kurkova**

# 11

---

# DAYS SPENT ALONE

There were many times as a child, that I was alone on the farm for several hours at a time. One way that I filled my time was to explore our woods. Even though I was only eight or nine, I was still allowed to go off on my own because there were few worries about anything happening to me. We didn't worry about wild animals or strange human beings. The time was just quiet and special.

On the lane that led back to the woods, there would be small pools of water. I would stop and watch the many tadpoles. They would only be tadpoles for a short time, but they were so peaceful to watch. After watching them for a time, I would go back to the woods. These were not ordinary woods. My father kept the grass mowed and the dead branches picked up. It looked more like a park. In the spring and summer the woods would be filled with all sorts of wild flowers. The colors and smells were magnificent. I enjoyed the solitude. There was also a couple of small ponds. One pond in particular had tree roots extending out over the water. I would sit there for hours watching a leaf float by or I would toss a pebble into the water and watch the ripples.

As a child, I thought I was lonely, but now I realize that I had the best of times. I learned to appreciate nature and quiet time. To this day, I don't mind being by myself and I actually enjoy the quiet times. I don't feel that I am a loner, but just alone with myself. This time has made me realize that I want to be surrounded only by people who appreciate what God has given us. I don't want people hurrying around me or worrying about tomorrow. God has made our surroundings for us to enjoy, not to destroy or ignore.

> *"Spend some time by yourself. Get to know who you are."* — **June Elaine**

# 12

## BEING PUT DOWN

Do you have a "friend" who likes, or enjoys, putting you down? They think that they are always right and don't value, or even listen to, your opinion on a subject. Worse yet, they don't let you finish a sentence. They think that they already know what you are going to say.

You know, YOU are just as important as they are. We are all God's children. We all have thoughts and dreams just like everyone else.

Are they insecure or jealous? It's hard at times, but this is when we should be the most patient and compassionate toward them. They may just be having a bad day. We all have them. Some of us control our emotions better than others. Just step back and breathe before letting words come out of your mouth that you can never take back.

> *"Don't be distracted by criticism. Remember*
> *— the only taste of success some people get*
> *is to take a bite out of you."* **–Zig Ziglar**

# 13

❧

## VACATION
## EXPERIENCE

Recently, a wonderful vacation and the chance to see a somewhat forbidden area crossed my path. I got to go to Havana, Cuba. In the process of going to this area, I was almost physically run down on the ship by another woman. In my mind, she was a "very pushy person." No consideration for another human was even thought of.

Later, by accident, I came face to face with her. I was very cautious in speaking to her. It turns out that she was very friendly and interesting. We had a great time sharing stories and learning about each other's lives.

We never know what is going on in someone's life. We have to be willing to give that person a chance. Listen to what they have to say, then interact with them. This "pushy person" turned out to be quite pleasant. Always keep an open mind.

*"Stay opened minded. Things aren't always what they seem to be."*

**—Scottie Waves**

*"Minds are like parachutes. They only function when they are open."*

**—Lord Thomas Robert Dewar**

# 14

❧

# STRESSFUL
# HOLIDAYS

For some, the holidays are not easy. Did a death occur around this time, or do you feel the pressure of buying gifts for other people even though you don't have the money to do so? People can even go into debt succumbing to the gift-giving pressure.

It can be a very stressful time. So many people forget the real reason that we celebrate Christmas. No matter what our beliefs are, we should be spiritually reflecting instead of rushing to buy the next present.

Take a moment to just breathe and know that the amount a gift costs or its size is not the important issue. Do something nice or bake something special for someone. Just show someone kindness of some kind. There are lots of people feeling the same pressure as us. It may be the best gift that you can give — to just be kind.

> *"Kindness is a gift everyone can afford to give."* **—Unknown**

# 15

## LIFE IS PRECIOUS

Life, as we know it, is precious. As little children, we can't wait to grow up and be on our own. THEN, we do grow up and the question is: what do we do now? We make our decisions, right or wrong, and assume our place in society. Sometimes we fit in. Other times we become independent and try our best to be different. Different is not bad, because different people tend to think for themselves. Some may think that we are just quiet or weird. I prefer to think of us as unique. There is only one person just like us, and that is us. We may set the world on fire with our thoughts and objectives. We may have to strike a match many times before we light that fire, but we have it in us. At times we don't even know it, but the fire is simmering just waiting to be become a bonfire and, then, an entire wall of flames.

My wall of fire didn't become a flame until much later in life. People kept kicking dirt on my fire. Just when I thought I could see a small spark, here came the dirt. This happened over and over until I became determined and said, "No more!"

I know that I have worth. I think that my gentleness is a blessing from God. One doesn't have to be loud or boisterous to become successful. Sometimes the gentle and unassuming are the ones that become the loudest through their achievements.

*"Everything you need to be great is already inside you. Stop waiting for someone or something to light your fire. YOU HAVE THE MATCH."* —**Darren Hardy**

# 16

## WHERE DO WE GO FROM HERE

We have all heard the saying "drop back and punt," but should we do that as seniors? Maybe our time now should be spent accepting our life, and enjoying our time. I know that Grandma Moses started painting in her nineties, but not all of us want to busy our lives more. We want to rest and enjoy life as seniors.

I have started writing as a senior, but I'm doing this as a cathartic, selfish act to understand my past. Putting feelings down on paper has been a wonderful release for me. It has helped me understand some of the "whys" in my past. Some of these have been revealed with sad emotions, and some have been informative.

We can't all have the perfect childhood, and very few of us do, but to try to understand the happenings in our early life is a big step toward understanding ourselves as adults. Why is my disposition like it is? What influenced my character? Why is my thought process what it is?

There are answers. I'm continually looking. I have found some comfort, but there are vast questions remaining.

Let's get to know ourselves.

> *"To know thyself is the beginning*
> *of all wisdom."* — **Aristotle**

# 17

## MAKE LEMONADE
## OUT OF LEMONS

You have heard it before: "Make lemonade out of lemons." This is easier said than done sometimes. We have the best intentions, but putting them into action is another thing. At times, we think that it is easier to feel sorry for ourselves and our situation.

I have those moments also. I am a sensitive person. I am proud of that. It's not always easy to make "lemonade." Being sensitive is not bad. I think that sensitive people see a different side of emotions than what other people do.

Pat yourself on the back for being sensitive and caring. It is a quality that we don't see much of these days.

The next time that you see lemons, think lemonade. YOU CAN DO IT, whatever it is that needs to be done.

*"When life hands you lemons—squeeze them like crazy and enjoy the ride to lemonade."* — **June Elaine**

# 18

## IS LIFE FAIR?

Life is not always fair. We work and we do our best, but then something takes place and we feel like we are going backwards. We are spinning our wheels and not getting ahead, or accomplishing what we set out to do.

Step back and look at the situation. Maybe we are going in the wrong direction. You know, it's not always easy to admit, but we can't always be right. Sometimes we reach a stalemate. Maybe we are supposed to go in a different direction or maybe we are being protected from a negative event.

We have to trust our instincts, but also be willing to look at all of the possibilities. Wait awhile and think of all the possible angles. We just might come up with an even better solution.

> *"Step back, breath, and evaluate the*
> *problem, and then react."* **— June Elaine**

# 19

---

# BECOMING
# A BUTTERFLY

I have always had a keen awareness of butterflies. Their delicacy, beauty, and kaleidoscope of colors make each one a work of art. They approach life unaware of their impression on the human species. They are also vulnerable, like us humans.

I have always seen myself as the caterpillar trying to become the butterfly. For most of my childhood, I was limited in the expressions of affection that I could give. "I love you," was not a household term. In fact, the only time that I remembered hearing that phrase from my parents was on their deathbeds. Pity that we didn't experience more love in our lives.

Hopefully this is not the case in your life. Let people know how you feel, in a nice way. Tell them that you love them and that you appreciate them. If you don't express your feelings now, it may be too late when you finally decide to.

When you next see a butterfly, look at the colors and at how delicate they are. Yes, we are delicate and vulnerable, just as they are, but we have more resources. God gave us the ability to think, express, and love.

> *"Just when the caterpillar thought the world was over, it became a butterfly."* — **Unknown**

# 20

## FLYING
## AND SOARING

Several times in my life, I have tried to fly and soar with my endeavors, but I was always discouraged or put down. But this is my time. I don't know what it will be yet, but I will be good, even great, at something.

My strength is coming from God. He knows my heart and He knows that I need to be good at something in order to become confident in myself. I have always felt that I was sort of good at many things, but now God knows that I want to be great at something, and He is going to walk beside me to accomplish that.

You will be great at something also. You will fly and soar. Be kind to yourself and explore the possibilities in your life.

We don't know what the future holds, but God will give us direction and purpose.

> *"The future belongs to those who believe in the beauty of their dreams."* —**Eleanor Rosevelt**

# 21

## WHAT LOVE HAS MEANT TO ME

What is love? When I was young, love to me was someone showing you attention and affection. I didn't know that this was just physical, at least most of the time. The first time a person gives us attention, we think that we are in love.

Now in my senior years, I know that LOVE is a shared feeling and consideration between two people. LOVE is being concerned for each others safety and well being. LOVE is nurturing and being supportive of each others endeavours. LOVE is listening to each other even though it may not be your opinion or viewpoint. LOVE is comforting and caring in the worst and best of times. LOVE is being there for each other, believing in each other. LOVE is a gift.

When there is mutual respect and confidence in each other, oh how beautiful life can be.

*"Love never gives up, never loses faith, is always hopeful, and endures through every circumstance."*
**— 1 Corinthians 13:7**

# 22

## DARKNESS AND LIGHT

Have you noticed that after the dark of night comes the light of day? This is what occurs in our life as well. The darkness seems so dark at times and we think that we will never see the light again. I have said, in the past, that there is light at the end of the tunnel, but is it a freight train coming toward me?

I have been through a lot. Many have been through a lot worse. There is hope and wonderful light at the end of the tunnel. There is life after troubles. We don't want to make a decision that would be a permanent solution to a temporary problem.

God has a plan for us. We just have to wait sometimes to see what the plan is, and that is not always easy.

> *"Even if you're on the right track, you'll get run over if you just sit there."* **— Will Rogers**

# 23

## MY WORLD

Have you ever wondered, "What is my place in this world, and how do I find it?" At times, our place in the world finds us and uncontrollable circumstances determine our world. We are born in a certain state or country and maybe that is where we are suppose to be. We move sometimes to accommodate a job or to support our partner. Finding ourselves in a circumstance like this, we often feel that we were forced into a situation, and it's not always easy to find ourselves and where we belong.

Finding a new church, the library, or a book club or even just talking to a person at the store, sometimes leads to another opportunity. We just have to give ourselves, and time, a chance.

One of my moves has taken me years to adjust to, but I wouldn't want to leave now. I just had to give it time.

> *"Reading a book just might open a new chapter in your life."* **– June Elaine**

# 24

HURT
BY A FRIEND

Have you been hurt by a "friend?" It happens so quickly that you don't know how to respond. This happened to me.

I play cards once a week. This has been a source of therapy for me and also a deterrent from the problems of the world. Being with other people has also helped me in coming back from physical and emotional issues.

There comes a time when a person has to preserve their emotional dignity and depart from the hurtful ways of others. Maybe they do have problems and you want to be there for them, but you also have to decide to do what is best for you. Maybe it is to distance yourself from the situation.

That is what I am going to do. I feel that it will be a relief for me, as I will not feel like I am walking on eggshells. I hope that the relationship that I have with the others involved won't suffer, but this is what I have to do. God will guide me.

*"Use pain as a stepping stone, not a campground."* — **Alan Cohen**

# 25

## LIFE OF A
## SENIOR-AGER

Do you ever feel that life has passed you by? From a woman's point of view, I have spent most of my adult life doing for and helping others.

When I was first married, I thought I was to take care of my husband. WRONG. We were supposed to grow together and learn how to make each other happy.

Then along come children. You cook, clean, run them to practice, take them to lessons, and go to school functions. On and on and on. You lose yourself.

Then comes the time when they are a little older and in school, and maybe you can get a part-time job to supplement their needs and desires. Sounds good, but days off and summer break brings a new kind of problem. They still disagree and fight and call you at work, over and over and over.

Then, almost magically, they graduate from school. Before you know it, they are getting married. You may still be working and learning to live with the empty nest, but soon you get AARP literature. Welcome to being a Senior-Ager. Once you come to terms with the life that has flown by, you start to realize that this is the best time of your life. You can watch TV when you want. You can go wherever you want. You can vacation when you want. Eat what you want. Sleep when you want. Listen to the music that you haven't heard in years.

There are wonderful things to look forward to in your senior life. Thank God that you have made it this far.

ENJOY YOURSELF—YOU DESERVE IT!!!!!

*"You can't help getting older, but you don't have to get old."* **— George Burns**

# 26

※

# WHY
# PROCRASTINATE?

Are you, or is someone else you know, a procrastinator? This is something that I have trouble with. In the past, I have never made New Year's resolutions because I didn't keep them. This year I did make one. I was determined not to procrastinate on things that needed to be done. Picking up the house has never been a problem, but cleaning, doing laundry, going to the store, going through the mail, cleaning the litter box, have been. Fun things are always easier to do.

We all have to find what works for us. I am getting so much better. Just once a day, I do something right away that could be put off until another time. Be proud of yourself for doing this. Don't procrastinate. It really does feel good.

> *"When there is a hill to climb, don't think that waiting will make it smaller."* **— Unknown**

# 27

## A Little About Me

I have been thinking about writing this for some time. A little more about me. I hope that this will be encouraging and uplifting to someone.

The last six years have been a roller coaster. I took care of my husband for four years, but then lost him to the horrible disease, cancer. Exactly two months later, I had a stroke. The doctors said that the stroke was most likely from the strain and stress of taking care of my husband. I was in the hospital and then rehab for that, but fortunately I was able to recover. I had to learn to walk, write, feed myself, brush my teeth, and many other things again. I was just getting my life back when a driver crossed the median and hit me head on. Of course, there were severe injuries and rehab again. That year I spent Christmas and New Year's in rehab. Then a few months later I had a knee replacement. Again rehab. Then I fell and broke my femur. Rehab for a month this time.

While all this was happening, I prayed. I knew that everything happens for a reason and that God has a plan.

I met a very special person and acquired my own place during this time. I will never physically be the same, but in a lot of ways, I am a better person today.

What I want to say is that you can overcome anything that you put your mind to, if you really want to. There is always someone who has it much worse than you. You just need to be strong and have the strength of a tiger and trust in God.

> *"Courage isn't having the strength to go on — it is going on when you don't have strength."* **—Napoleon Bonaparte**

# 28

TELL YOUR
PAST OFF

"Okay," you say, "How do I tell my past off?" I don't have a definitive answer for you. I just know that we have to do it to move forward.

I was raised in a religion that taught me to be submissive. Being told what to do and when to do it were the norm. Maybe you can relate? Having strict parents, and a long list of rules wasn't easy. Don't wear slacks. Don't go to the movies. Don't dance. Don't play cards. Don't drink and, heaven forbid, if you had any interest in the opposite sex, don't engage in any sexual activity!

Loving actions, compliments, and encouragement were rare. When I did receive attention, it was flattering and so welcomed. I was starved for recognition and when I got it, it was exhilarating. When a young man stole my heart, I was blind to the big red flags that were right in front of my face. At first, it was very exciting, but then quiet control took over.

From moving to another town, to leaving all my friends, to being pulled away from my religion and being the sole support system for my husband while he pursued college and golf and his own social network, I slowly lost myself. I had quit my job and he lost his the week before our wedding. Married with no income wasn't fun, but I stuck it out, thinking it would get better.

The red flags were all there. I simply didn't see them. And today I forgive myself for that. You can too. You have to tell the past off. Forgive yourself. Only then can the future be bright and happy.

*"Today is the first day of the rest of you life."* **—Charles Dederich**

# 29

# TRAFFIC

Have you ever been upset with traffic? I just recently went out of town for a few days. I had a wonderful time—except when I was in traffic. Is there one individual that owns the highway? Isn't there ever a need for an individual to have compassion or even care that someone may not know a particular highway and they are watching signs? The honking, hand gestures (you know what I mean), and the words that come from people's mouths. It's almost like they leave their body and become this possessed creature.

I understand that someone might be running late for work or an appointment. LEAVE EARLIER! Even if a person is late for something, is it worth the race and chase if you die or are injured from an accident or maybe even injure someone else?

Let's think just a little and put ourselves in the other person's place. Be patient and, yes, leave a little earlier.

> *"Instead of putting others in their place, put yourself in their place."* — **Amish Proverb**

# 30

## RELATIVES

D o you have relatives that you don't understand? God made you all a family to enjoy, love, support, and just be there for each other in good times and bad. Yes, we all have minds and ideas of our own, but that doesn't mean that we shouldn't listen and respect the viewpoints of others. Be there for your family. We all need support at times.

Right or wrong, we shouldn't judge or question someone else until we have walked in their shoes.

> *"You don't choose your family. They are God's gift to you, as you are to them."* **—Desmond Tutu**

# 31

# FEELING DOWN?

We all have days when we feel a little down. What do we do? I know what we should do—go outside, call a friend, exercise, go shopping—these are just a few ideas. It's not always easy to make ourselves do the things that we know we should do.

You know what I have decided? It's not so bad to have a down day. Sometimes we are able to reflect more and look at our lives from a different angle. If someone is always happy and always doing the right thing, something is usually wrong in their life. How can someone have a perfect life?

I do believe in quiet times for ourselves. This is not all bad. If we learn to be alone with our thoughts, then we have a clearer mind to deal with others and day-to-day matters. Find your quiet place and enjoy your thoughts and accomplishments. We are unique human beings. Savor that blessing.

> *"Sometimes you have to take a step back*
> *to see that you're moving forward in*
> *the right direction."* **— Unknown**

# 32

## TO LOVE AND BE LOVED

To love and to be loved is the most amazing feeling. I didn't know what real love was for many years. I was acting out love.

I did love my children with everything that I had. I wanted to be an example to my children and grandchildren. I wanted them to see a strong, confident person. You can't tell them how to be strong and confident, but you can show them.

Life offers so much. We can be complacent and just survive day to day. But we need to reach higher, and out of our comfort zones. We need to dream. God has given us so much to enjoy, but I think that we take our daily lives for granted.

Watch the sunset, smell the flowers, enjoy the people and even the animals in your life.

> *"Show love in all that you do. When you show love, you receive love in return."* **– Unknown**

# 33

HANDLING
DEATH

When a friend dies, what should we do? It is hard to know what to do, and sometimes we do nothing. I have been guilty of this on several occasions. What do we say to convey how we feel or what words should we say that will comfort the survivor?

After personally going through this life-changing experience, I know that having someone just say, "Are you okay?" is so comforting. Just a hug, or asking if there is something that you can do, is so welcomed.

The one left behind is confused and bombarded with decisions to make. Just a smile or an invitation to go to lunch is an answer to a prayer.

Don't worry if you are saying the right words. Just be there and give your shoulder for them to cry on.

*"Death leaves a heartache no one can heal, but love leaves a memory that no one can steal."* **— Unknown**

# 34

CHILDHOOD
MEMORIES

Today I have been reminiscing, thinking about my past experiences with my two older brothers. I don't remember a lot about them as they were eleven and fourteen years older than me. The younger brother left for college at age sixteen, then the army, and then marriage. My oldest brother, after high school, was in the service and then married. They probably had experiences that I never heard about and I didn't think to ask them at the time. Now that they have passed away, I can think of many questions.

Think about your childhood. Where did your name come from? How did your siblings respond to another "pesky" sibling coming into their life? Ask why they made the decisions for their lives that they made.

Take advantage of this time to learn more about your past and what led to NOW. It might even be a chance to get closer to your siblings and enjoy each other.

> *"Side by side or miles apart, we are siblings connected by the heart."* **— Unknown**

# 35

※

# Friends Moving
# To A New Area

A good friend is moving. I really hate to see this happen, but it is a wonderful new chapter in her life. However, you tend to think that a good friend of yours will be around forever.

In today's world of opportunities, we never know when a change is about to happen. This friend is moving about thirteen hundred miles away. Several years ago, that would seem like a lifetime away. Today, it is just a short plane commute. I don't know if we will see each other again, but we will definitely keep in touch.

Leaving family and friends will be traumatic for her, but she is going back to other family, a new house, and a new job. How exciting to be able to have a fresh, new start.

Be there for your friend and wish them the best life ever. Congratulate them on this opportunity.

*"Even when someone is miles away, always remember this: we are under the same sky looking at the same sun, moon and stars."* **— Unknown**

# 36

## LONELINESS

Loneliness is a complicated thing. Some people are lonely because they choose to be. They don't associate with other humans by choice. Some people are lonely because they have been forgotten by their family. Some are lonely because "friends" see them as a threat to their egos. They wouldn't want to be seen with someone using a walker or a cane. Most of these lonely people have interesting words to communicate, but no one to listen to them.

In this age of technology, a phone call is just a second away. We don't even need to write a letter (what's that?), but even sending a card letting someone know that you are thinking of them is appreciated. Buying several cards at a time, to have on hand, is convenient so you can send a card whenever you are thinking of that person.

We all need to be better at this simple courtesy. Something so simple can make a real difference in someone's life. We may not even realize that someone is lonely and we just may be in that situation ourselves one day.

> *"Loneliness and the feeling of being unwanted is the most terrible poverty."* —**Mother Teresa**

# 37

## HEALTH ISSUES

What do you do when the doctor makes you feel like the most unhealthy person around? Lose weight, lower your cholesterol, exercise more. Are you depressed? Well, I am now. Most of us try our best, but should we deprive ourselves constantly? We eat our salads, and veggies, and fruit, and lean meat, but sometimes our genetics play a big part in our biological makeup.

Doctors have to answer to someone too. They are sometimes connected to medical regulations and have to answer to government rules. I know that they have to ask "the questions," but do they have to make us feel anxious and scared?

Maybe they should show more compassion. But, do they have the time? They are under pressure also. I am not putting all doctors in this category. Some doctors are very concerned about our well-being and take their time with us.

Let's do our best to be healthy. After all, we are just passing through this life. When we reach our "Home" no one will be worrying about any of these issues.

> *"The best investment you can ever make*
> *is in your own health."* **— Unknown**

# 38

---

# BUMPS
# IN THE ROAD
# OF LIFE

"Bumps in the road." In life, we all have them. Yesterday I had a day that had several bumps. I went to the doctor's office to pick up some medicine. It was closed, even though it was supposed to be open. Then I went to the bank to use the ATM— it was down. I went home to activate a credit card, the company's computer system was down. Then a phone call revealed that I would have to get blood work every day until further notice—every day. This would mean traveling several miles each day and canceling other appointments that had already been made. Needless to say, at this point, I was somewhat upset.

We all have these days. How we handle them is what sets us apart from others. I sat down, took some deep breaths, and started thinking about the positives in my life. I even ended up laughing hysterically with a friend. In Proverbs, God said, "a cheerful heart is good medicine." By the end of the day, I felt great. The "bumps" were behind me. Tomorrow is another day, hopefully one with no bumps.

*"God put bumps in the road — to keep us from falling asleep at the wheel."* **— Unknown**

# 39

## BIRTHDAYS

Birthdays. They come too often. I know that birthdays only happen once a year, but the time just flies. So many people say that they aren't going to have any more birthdays, but I WANT to keep having them — the more the better.

I just had a birthday. I can't believe that I am the age that I am. I would say to you—enjoy your time. Do the things that you have been putting off. Travel if you want. Make contact with an old friend. Try to make things right with someone whom you have had a disagreement with. My saying is "put the ball in their court." A year later, the ball may still be in their court, but at least you tried.

Celebrate having another birthday. You never know how many more you will have.

*"Know that you are the perfect age. Each year is special and precious, for you shall only live it once. Be comfortable with growing older."* — **Louise Hay**

# 40

## FINDING MY LAST LOVE

Finding my last love. Does this sound silly or impossible? It can happen and it did happen for me. I was talked into joining an online dating service. I decided that I would just do it to make my friend happy. I joined for one month. Guess what? I did meet someone. My rules were kind of rigid, because I thought this was just a fun and temporary thing to do. I met someone who was so very easy to talk to, very understanding, and looking for a gentle and lasting relationship. He has become my best friend. We can talk about, literally, anything. We laugh a lot.

He is so supportive of any endeavor I might attempt and always motivates me to try new challenges. I wish that I would have met him years ago. Maybe I would have made more of my life. My past has made me who I am today, so I guess I met him at just the right time. We have a very loving, gentle, and happy relationship. We have a great understanding of each other. We accept each other, imperfections and all. We love each other unconditionally.

We all have skeletons in our past, but the past is the past. Leave it there and move on. Life is so short and so precious that we need to make the most of each day. What are we waiting for? We have to make our desired future happen, not just sit around and wait for something to come to us.

*"Enjoy the life that God has given you."* **— June Elaine**

# 41

---

## OBSESSED
## FOR ATTENTION

Do you know someone who is obsessed with getting attention? This is not an easy situation to deal with. They often embellish their stories to make themselves look better, or sometimes worse, to get attention. This reminds me of the story "The Boy Who Cried Wolf." You get to the point where you don't pay attention to them because you don't know what is real. They always do something better, or bigger, or more often than you. I honestly believe that they don't know how to be honest or relay a true circumstance or feeling.

We have to be tolerant of this, even though it certainly is not easy. We have to make our own decisions for how to react to this behavior.

Smiling or humming has been my "go to" reaction. Sometimes not saying anything is the best answer. (Also try this with your children. It makes them wonder what Mom is really thinking.)

> *"Before you react, think. Before you spend, earn. Before you criticize, wait. Before you quit, try."* — **Earnest Hemmingway**

# 42

## FRIDAYS

Maybe it's just me, but it seems like everything is different on a Friday. I don't like to get the mail on Friday because there is always a bill, or a letter letting me know of a problem, or worse yet, something has been canceled. Getting hold of a doctor on a Friday is almost impossible. Are we just not supposed to get sick on a Friday? Does the Hippocratic Oath still cover a doctor's obligations on a Friday?

You probably can guess by now that I have been sick. I am better now thanks to the help of God, the advice of trained loved ones, and conclusions made on my part. After contacting a doctor's office Friday morning at 9:00, I received a call back the following Monday morning and was told to go to the emergency room. Thank goodness, I already felt better.

Hopefully, this was an isolated incident. We have to think for ourselves and come to our own conclusions at times. Do our own investigating. We have to make sure that we are informed of and know about medications and procedures. Several years ago, a doctor told me to look at the plaque on his wall. It stated that he was in the "practice" of medicine; he was not perfect. We have to remember this.

*"Thinking is the hardest work there is,
which is probably the reason why so
few engage in it."* — **Henry Ford**

# 43

POWER WASH
OUR LIFE

The other day, the management company for my complex had someone power washing my building. I got to thinking — wouldn't it be nice if we could just power wash our life? If we could just wash away everything that we didn't like or that went wrong in our life? Wouldn't it be refreshing to say goodbye to those negative happenings?

Who we are today is because of our past and we are the positive product of everything that has taken place. Most of the time, we are too hard on ourselves, myself included.

Pat yourself on your back. We can handle whatever comes our way. God doesn't give us more than what we can handle. HE LOVES US THAT MUCH.

> *"We are all here for some special reason. Stop being a prisoner of your past. Become the architect of your future."* **— Robin Sharma**

# 44

## Dreams

Dreams. We all have them, but it's not always easy to reach for them. My website has given me the courage to try something else that I have always dreamed of. I am going to write a book. You noticed that I didn't say that I was going to try, or that I was thinking about it. I AM going to do this. It may take me some time, but it will happen.

The other morning I woke up with a title and the first sentence of my book in my thoughts. It just kept repeating over and over in my mind, so I got up and went to the computer. I will keep writing my thoughts and memories. It will all come together at some point.

Don't be afraid to try. I've waited so long to try something new. We can do this. We may have setbacks, but let's keep moving forward. As I have said before—don't look back. You are not going that way.

> *"I walk slowly, but I never walk backward."* — **Abraham Lincoln**

# 45

## HONESTY

Honesty is a word that is not prevalent in a lot of people's vocabulary anymore. Sometimes it is hard to be honest, but it is so appreciated by most. It seems that it is better to be honest about a situation than to have the other person involved thinking negative thoughts.

Integrity and honesty are virtues that make a person who they are. I have known people that lie even when they didn't need to. I think that they have lied so many times that they don't know how to be truthful and honest. I'm not sure what to do in this circumstance. Do we confront the person or do we forget it?

We must always be honest ourselves and be an example. Maybe by being an example, they will see that honesty doesn't hurt and that it is a virtue. It certainly is appreciated.

*"The foundation stones for a balanced success are honesty, character, integrity, faith, love and loyalty."* **— Zig Ziglar**

# 46

SEASONS
OF LIFE

We are all in a different season of life and we never know what is just around the corner. Worry, concern, relationships, health, and issues of all dimensions can change our lives. We never know what the next day might bring. Yet, we are better human beings because of our past. The future and the events that will unfold will also better us as human beings. We will be wiser, and we will know that if we have handled the past, that we CAN handle the future.

Most likely, we have all had struggles of one kind or another. Life certainly doesn't seem perfect. Some days are harder than others, but let the past be in the past, and we will move forward.

> *"Life is too short to be anything*
> *but happy."* **— Unknown**

# 47

## FEELINGS

We always have to be considerate of other people's feelings, but we also still have to be ourselves. We have to convey how we feel, whether it is right or wrong.

There are people who delight in saying hurtful things. I don't feel that they are being themselves. I just think that they want and need the attention. They have most likely been hurt by someone themselves. Some people are bitter and angry from something that has happened in their past. They are lashing out at anyone near them.

There are also times that we don't dare say what we are thinking. Some things are better left unsaid.

> *"Be who you are and say what you feel because those who mind don't matter, and those who matter don't mind."* **— Bernard Bauch**

# 48

## My Way
## or the Highway

"My way or the highway." Have you ever heard that before? So many people feel that "their" way is the only way to accomplish something. That is far from the truth. In almost every circumstance there is more than one way to do something. There is more than one way to get to a location, more than one way to shop, or to clean. Then there is cooking. You can try to make any certain dish in so many different ways.

I was told as a child that there was only one way to get to heaven and that was by belonging to a certain denomination. I know now that isn't true. Every religion is trying to get to heaven, just in different ways.

Develop your own way of doing things. What is right for one person is not always right for another. Develop YOUR way. That is what makes you unique. We are all unique people. Embrace it.

> *"A pessimist sees the difficulty in every opportunity. The optimist sees the opportunity in every difficulty."* **— Sir Winston Churchill**

# 49

## STORMS

We all have a storm in our life, whether it is in the past or is just now brewing. Sometimes that storm is within ourselves. Problems are sometimes forced upon us and other times we may feel like the torrential aggravation will never end.

JUST BREATHE. At some point, as in all storms, the disturbance will go away. We tend to get so emotionally involved that we don't take time to step back and look at the whole picture.

There seems to always be a calm after a storm. Learn from the lightning and thunder—and don't forget to breathe.

*"In life, storms come not to hurt you, but to make you stronger."* **— Debasish Mridha**

# 50

***

## COMMUNICATION

Did you flunk the "Mind Reading" course? I did. There are people who automatically think that you know what they mean, even when they don't actually say it. This can cause so many problems. You may think that you hear what they are saying, but what you think might be the opposite of what they really mean.

Communication is becoming a lost art. I feel that people have become so dependent on technology that they don't know how to communicate. We have to be able to say what we are thinking, but in a nice way, so that the other person understands what we mean. Thoughts and communication are being lost to the cell phone or the computer.

Remember, we can't read the minds of others and they can't read ours. It is kind of scary though with artificial intelligence (AI) on the rise. There may come a time when mind reading will be the norm. I guess that we will just have to be careful of what we are thinking when that time comes. LOL!

> *"People can't hear what you don't say. Thinking is not communicating."* — **Frank K. Sonnenberg**

# 51

## CLOUDS

We have had plenty of dark clouds lately. Storms or rain almost every day. Some people only ever see dark clouds though. They are always pessimistic instead of being optimistic. Sometimes all that you hear from them are negative words. You know that their life is even more miserable because they only see the dark clouds.

There are good and positive moments in every situation. Even if you meet a person that is dressed really "creatively," you still might see the pretty and interesting colors that they have on. I will admit that I have seen some newborn babies that weren't so cute, but they are always so sweet and what a blessing to have this gift from God. A POSITIVE statement.

Try to always find something good and positive in everything. It's not always easy. If we just stop and think of what we would like to have said to us, we just might see the sun peeking out through those dark clouds.

*"Once you replace negative thoughts*
*with positive ones, you'll start having*
*positive results."* — **Willie Nelson**

# 52

## UNCONDITIONAL LOVE

If people would only love as unconditionally as some animals do, what a great world we would have. Animals don't care about physical inabilities. They don't care if our clothes don't match. They don't care if we live in a place with one room or ten rooms. They just care about us.

Yes, we do have to provide for them; they depend on that. We have to give them food and water. We walk them or keep their litter box clean. In return they "just love" us.

If only people would "just love." Most people have conditions attached to their love. We see this in government, marriage, friendships, and general relationships. A lot of these conditions are motivated by people's own desires.

Back to animals. My cat inspired me to write this. Taffy is her name. She watches out for me. If I leave, she comes running to the door to greet me when I get back. She loves and accepts me unconditionally. Animals hear the voice of God and are happy to just be. Hopefully, the rest of the world will learn from animals.

*"Unconditional love is the greatest gift of all."* **— Sylvia Messara**

# 53

## LIFE IS LIKE
## SOLITAIRE

L ife is like solitaire. We play the hand that we are dealt. Sometimes we win, and sometimes we lose. We play it alone, but we keep playing.

I have played this card game many times, but never before thought of it as like my life. Some days we win in our endeavors. Other days it seems like everything goes wrong, no matter how hard we try.

Never give up though. The next move just might be the one that changes your life.

*"Never give up, for that is just the place and time that the tide will turn."* — **Harriet Beecher Stowe**

# 54

## LOVE YOURSELF

The size of your house doesn't make a difference (to most people). The size of your car doesn't matter either. So, why does the size of YOU matter to some people? After spending most of my life being called chubby, overweight, large-framed, and big, I have come to the conclusion that dealing with extra weight is sometimes just hereditary. I don't have anything to back up that theory, just my own feelings. Being reasonable about what we put into our bodies, eating healthy, exercising (not my best virtue), appreciating who we are, and respecting ourselves is the most important thing.

What if I am a size fourteen, sixteen, or larger? What if I wear extra large tops? What I am on the outside does not determine what I am on the inside.

Learn to love yourself and know that YOU are a wonderful contribution to this world. Beauty is not a size.

*"Confidence is beautiful, no matter your size, no matter your weight. Be confident in who you are and you will be beautiful."* **— Unknown**

# 55

❧━━━◆━━━❧

# INCONSIDERATE
PEOPLE

Inconsiderate people are all around us, but an inconsiderate business is hard to accept. How do they expect to stay in business if they don't practice the Golden Rule? Keeping an appointment, or doing what they said they would do, should be the priority.

I don't think that I am the only one experiencing this. I do have a solution to offer you though. Don't act immediately. Think about the situation and come up with a plan that makes YOU look like the rational one. There is an old saying—you can catch more flies with honey than you can with vinegar. Be sweet in your response. It makes you feel better knowing that you have been cool, calm, and collected. Hmmmmmm—Easy? No. Necessary? Yes. Our pride gets in the way at times.

*The Golden Rule—"Do unto others as you would have them do unto you."* **— Matthew 7- 12**

# 56

## LISTENING

Do you really listen when you hear? So much of the time we aren't actually listening and we are thinking about something else. A person doesn't just talk to hear themselves. They are saying something that they want you to hear, so listen carefully.

A real pet peeve of mine is when I am talking and someone cuts me off. Don't be afraid to, in a nice way, say, " Would you mind letting me finish what I was saying?" Why do other people assume that they know what you are going to say?

Be courteous of others and don't interrupt them. We don't always realize that we do this. Make sure that you are LISTENING.

> *"Give every man thy ear, but few thy voice."* — **William Shakespeare**

> *"God gave us mouths that close and ears that don't. That must tell us something."* — **Unknown**

*57*

## STRESS

Stress is a word that can be used for many situations. I don't even know how to describe stress, but I just know when I am dealing with it. And right now, I am. True, this is not a life and death stressful situation; I am only getting new carpet. However, the preparation is not easy, and especially not for a somewhat handicapped person.

We are all faced with a stressful situation at some point in our lives. It's how we handle it that makes the difference. I have mentioned it before —but, we have to breathe and say to ourselves, "This too shall pass."

It's hard to look beyond the stress that we are experiencing, but we will make it through and most of the time we bring the stress on ourselves. God doesn't give us more than we can handle, but sometimes WE DO.

*"Relax, Breathe.....then React."* **— June Elaine**

# 58

## RAINY DAYS

We all have those days. I'll call them rainy days. It seems like the sun will never shine. The thunder gets louder and the lightning comes bolting across the sky. We don't know what to do or where to turn.

You know, the sun doesn't shine every day, but it doesn't rain everyday either. Let's get better at taking the bad with the good. The "good" is just around the corner. We WILL find the sun again.

*"With the new day comes new strength and new thoughts."* **— Eleanor Roosevelt**

*59*

# Knowledge

We are always going to meet someone who has obtained more knowledge then we have. Does that make us less of a person? Of course not. We are all individuals and have been made by the Master. We all have our thoughts and ideas, and they will always be ours. We have been given the ability to think and to determine our own thoughts.

Hopefully, we will always continue to learn and mentally produce new ideas and put those ideas into action.

We have to learn to be the best that we can be. If we are happy and content with our own selves, the people around us will also be happy and content. BE YOURSELF.

> *"Never interrupt someone doing something you said couldn't be done."* — **Amelia Earhart**

# 60

## BEING MISUNDERSTOOD

B eing misunderstood is an unfortunate happening. People don't always give us the chance to explain ourselves and, sometimes, just "being" gives off a certain persona that is misunderstood.

I have been told that I sometimes seem distant, uncaring, prim, and proper. The fact is, I am quiet, soft spoken, and somewhat shy. I don't feel that I need to be loud, or domineering, or controlling. Remember what we were told as kids — you are to be seen and not heard.

Maybe we are all misunderstood at times. We just have to be true to ourselves and how we feel. Just always remember—the ones who matter don't care, and the ones who care don't matter. As long as you understand yourself, that is all that matters.

> *"I'm only responsible for what I say, not for what you understand."* **— Unknown**

# 61

RAIN
IN OUR LIFE

It's raining here right now. There are all kinds of rain in our life. Some are emotional, some are physical, some are natural. Natural rain is a pleasant way to relax. The surroundings look greener and the air smells wonderful.

When there is emotional or physical rain to deal with, we often can only see the storms and can't see through the raindrops to see the beauty around us. Sometimes the rain only lasts for a few minutes. Other times it seems like the rain will never stop, but then we see a rainbow in the sky, and our life gets brighter.

Wait out the rain before making decisions. Stop and take time to see the beauty around you and smell the fresh air. It may be raining today, but tomorrow the sun may be shining, even brighter than you imagined.

> *"Rain may dampen your life, but rain WILL dry up and go away."* — **June Elaine**

# 62

---

# TECHNICAL "EXPERTS"

I t is so annoying when dealing with computer "experts." They think that everyone has the same level of computer experience as them. They rattle off computer terms that I have never heard of, and that I'm not so sure I even want to know. I am a "hands-on" person. If I can do something myself, or at least see it being done, then, and only then, can I understand and remember. Hopefully I am not the only person who takes this approach to a situation.

If you are someone who is very knowledgeable about computers, please have patience with us who don't know. I asked someone recently to speak MY language (not computer language) and to please slow down. In a nice way, of course.

We all can't know everything about every subject. But, there are classes available on almost everything. I guess I need to better myself in this computer area. Let's all try to better ourselves. Recently, I have been using the local library more. There are books on every subject and the people who work there are so helpful.

Don't limit yourself. We have to continue to "learn" and "bloom."

*"That some achieve great success is proof to all that others can achieve it as well."* — **Abraham Lincoln**

# 63

## UNPLANNED HAPPENINGS

I made an unplanned visit to the hospital. (I guess most of the time hospital visits are not planned.) Everything is fine, but I learned several lessons. First, most people are very nice if you are nice. If you smile, they will smile. No one wants to be a patient in the hospital, but I am so glad that the hospital, doctors, and nurses are there.

The paramedics were also very nice and they taught me an important lesson. I had never called them before for myself. Not only were they so nice, they also kindly reprimanded me for not calling them sooner. They stated that they were there to help and that health events can change in a second, SO NEVER WAIT.

Never hesitate to talk to the nurses and other people working in the hospital. I have a feeling that most patients do not seem interested in these people. They have worked hard and have sacrificed to get where they are. They have done this because they want to make people better and be there to help you.

God brought me through this event with a plan in mind.

*"Kind words can be short and easy to speak, but their echoes are truly endless."* — **Mother Teresa**

# 64

## Blooming

We look at a flower garden. We see an array of beautiful colors and different types of flowers. Look at these flowers as people. We are all different shapes and colors. Flowers don't all bloom at the same time, and neither do we. Just don't give up on yourself or someone else. Sometimes it is hard to encourage someone else if we don't feel encouraged ourselves. Time is our friend.

The Cirrus Cactus blooms only at night and only once a year, but it is beautiful when it blooms. We will be beautiful when we bloom. We just have to be patient with others, flowers, .....and ourselves.

> *"You need to be patient in order to do the will of God and receive what He promises."* — **Hebrews 10- 36 (GNT)**

# 65

## KNOWING

I f we knew then what we know now, then we wouldn't have done half of what we did. How many times have we thought this? We didn't have the wisdom, or the knowledge, then to know how something was going to affect our lives.

We are who we are today because of the past. Yes, we probably would have made some different decisions, but why second guess ourselves? We did what we thought was best at the time.

Be proud of who you are and what you have accomplished. If you want to accomplish more, GET BUSY. We don't know what we CAN do until we DO it, or at least try.

> *"What we have gone through brought us*
> *to where we are now."* **— Unknown**

# 66

## OUR
## FEELINGS

We can't always control our heart and our feelings, but sometimes our mind and logic must overrule our heart and our feelings. We may feel a certain way, but logic has to play a part in our actions. A certain action, or reaction, may not be in our best interest. Feelings of the heart are almost instant and instinctual. We must think the situation through and then decide the outcome.

The old saying, "stop and count to ten" may be the wisest thing to do. Just giving ourselves the chance to think about the situation sometimes renders a whole different outcome.

We don't always have the perfect answer, but WE ARE NOT PERFECT. Don't be too hard on yourself.

> *"Never make permanent decisions based on temporary feelings."* **— Unknown**

# 67

## MAKING MONEY STRETCH

Money just doesn't seem to ever go far enough. It seems to disappear. When I had two incomes to work with, it did seem a little easier, but now with one income, it is a challenge at times.

I had to adopt a phrase in my life— do I "want" something or do I "need" it? Of course, I can't buy everything that I want. We have to decide what is most important in our life. Certainly, an expensive purse or an article of clothing would not take priority over food for our family. At least, it shouldn't. A lot of people get carried away with their wants, at the expense of their needs.

Let's be reasonable. Most of us will not win the lottery. Even just playing the lottery may take money away from our needs. We just have to work with what we have and BUDGET for what we need.

> *"We must consult our means rather than our wishes."* **— George Washington**

# 68

## GOALS

Don't let anyone stand in the way of your goals. Someone is always going to come along and try to knock you down, or try to make you think that you can't accomplish what you set out to do. Listen to your heart and mind. We were given a brain so that we could think for ourselves. Granted, there are circumstances that always have to be considered, but we were created to think for ourselves and to be productive.

We can overcome many obstacles—I know I have. We have to be warriors, or a Pegasus, and fly and soar. Don't ever let anyone put down your ideas and thoughts. Where would our world be today if the inventors, scientists, mathematicians, and other great thinkers, would have listened to the doubts of people around them?

We all have times of uncertainty. Just don't give up on your dreams. YOU CAN MAKE YOUR DREAMS COME TRUE.

> *"Logic will get you from A to B. Imagination will take you everywhere."* **— Albert Einstein**

> *"Learn from yesterday, live for today, hope for tomorrow. The important thing is not to stop questioning."* **— Albert Einstein**

# 69

FEELINGS
FROM THE PAST

J ust when we have taken several steps forward, a feeling from the past creeps back in. We can't expect to just completely clear all bad memories and experiences from our minds. We can learn to recognize these negative feelings and lay them to rest and focus on all of the positives in our lives.

If our past has been far from perfect, I think that these memories will come back. However, we must not dwell on the past. The future can be what we want it to be. Nothing in life is perfect. Some people may appear to have everything, and maybe they do as far as material things are concerned, but NO ONE has a perfect situation in life.

I am writing this because I also deal with this scenario. No one is exempt.

> *"Everyday can't be honey. Some days are sour. How we handle the sour makes the honey even sweeter."* — **June Elaine**

# 70

## OUR
## UNIVERSE

Our universe gives us so many beautiful objects to look at and witness. Take the moon, for instance. Have you ever been outside at night and looked at the moon? You know, it is sometimes hard to imagine that the whole world sees the same moon.

What I like most about looking at the moon is that it is usually done at a quiet and peaceful time of night and we can just look directly up at the moon. We can erase our minds of all other thoughts and just look at the peaceful spectacle in the sky. We don't dare look directly at the sun, and besides, when the sun is out, it is a busy, hectic, noisy time of the day.

We all need to relax more and enjoy the quiet times. It seems like our lives are so rushed and that the hustle bustle is happening all around us.

Even if it is only for five minutes a day, indulge yourself and find that quiet time…..just for you.

> *"And if you are ever feeling lonely, just look at the moon. Someone, somewhere is looking at it too."* **— Unknown**

# 71

## SCARS

Visible scars on a person are always sad. We wonder how they came to be when we see them. Did someone have a bad accident, a bad physical encounter with a person or animal, or endure something even worse?

We all have scars. Some are visible and some are not. Some of us have both kinds. We can learn to live with visible scars, but sometimes the invisible ones are harder to deal with. Recent scars often bring feelings quickly to the surface, but soon they become a little less consuming. It only takes a word or some incident to affect us in an emotional way.

We can overcome these negative feelings. I didn't say that they would go away. But by redirecting our thoughts and doing new things, we will not only be improving ourselves, we just might discover that we really enjoy doing something new —AND are really good at it.

*"Why do we close our eyes when we pray, cry, kiss, dream? Because the most beautiful things in life are not seen, but felt only with the heart."* **— Anonymous**

# 72

## BEING
## HEALTHY

Eating has always been an issue for me. Being raised on a farm, food was prepared for working on the farm. Lots of meat, potatoes, vegetables that were often creamed, and noodles were always on the menu. There was a lot of physical work. Although I no longer experience the day-to-day rigors of farm life, adjusting my eating habits to match a more sedentary lifestyle has been a challenge.

I have tried to adapt to the saying, "eat to live, don't live to eat." Eating healthy is not always a "want," but a "need." As I am getting older, I can't digest some foods as easily as I used to. Isn't this a bummer?

I think that I have tried every diet. I have finally realized that just being reasonable and healthy is what we should strive for. Do I cut out desserts? No, but I do limit them. My desire for sugar has lessened a great deal. Some foods are "red flags." I don't dare have ice cream in the house. I don't even go down that aisle at the grocery store.

Be sensible and do what is HEALTHY FOR YOU. As you have probably heard—you are what you eat.

> *"Here's to better habits, positive thinking, clean eating and most of all — LOVING YOURSELF."* **— Unknown**

# 73

## SUCCESS

Success is measured in many ways and in many categories. Some people are successful in business, some in relationships, and some people are successful in day-to-day life. Some days success can be just getting the laundry done.

We tend to think of success in a monetary way, but that can be a delusion. Just because someone has lots of money, or many business ventures, may not mean that they are successful and happy in their private life.

Let's look at each day and tell ourselves what our success of that day is. It may be to finish reading a book, or to call a friend, making a special meal, or baking cookies for the kids when they get home from school. A good day at work could be your success. A quiet day with your significant other could be your success.

WE ARE ALL SUCCESSFUL IN MANY WAYS. Dream, plan, and get busy.

> *"When everything seems to be going against you, remember—an airplane takes off against the wind, not with it."* **— Henry Ford**

# 74

---

## YOU ARE SPECIAL

An uninterrupted good night's sleep is so rewarding. You can wake up with a new perspective and new outlook on life for whatever situation you might be in. With a clear head and rested mind, problems seem smaller. Decisions seem easier to make. We can't always follow through on those decisions right away, but we can decide on a course which we can then plan for and work towards.

Life isn't easy at times, but don't forget yourself. Do something special for yourself. After all, YOU ARE SPECIAL. God made you unique. There is no one else like you.

> *" A good laugh and a long sleep are the two best cures for anything. "* — **Irish Proverb**

# 75

## HOLIDAYS

Can you believe that the holidays are just around the corner? Hopefully you will be able to spend quality time with your family.

If we are lucky, we have family close by to celebrate with. If we can't be with our family, make someone else's holiday special. So many people are forgotten, especially in nursing homes.

All of the holidays have become so commercial. Many people have forgotten the real meaning of each holiday.

Bring back old traditions or start new ones for you and your family. Make memories that will never be forgotten.

> *"When purchasing gifts becomes the focal point of the season, we lose focus on what's truly important."* — **Joshua Fields Millburn**

# 76

## ACCEPTANCE

I hope that you are having a "sun-filled" day. Smile and think positive thoughts. We tend to let negative thoughts creep in at times. There is something good in everything. It's not always easy to find the "good," but it is there.

Be good to yourself; you are "special." God made you different from anyone else in the world. Don't try to be like someone else.

My friend is the smartest person I have ever known. He speaks several languages, is a physicist, author, and a recording artist. And he is also very sensitive and so very caring. At first, I felt inferior, but not anymore. I can do things that he can't. I am unique, just as he is. God made us different to accomplish His plan, not ours.

Be the best that you can be in your own way. We have to ACCEPT, DEFINE, and REFINE who WE are.

*"Being positive won't guarantee you'll succeed. But being negative will guarantee you won't."* — **J. Gordon**

# 77

## FEARS

The fear of going over a bridge is very real. I know, as I have had this fear for years. Some people think this fear is just imaginary. It's not, and my fear is much better now as I have worked on it.

One time several years ago, our family was taking a road trip. I was asleep in the front seat as a panicked feeling came over me. I woke up to find that we were going over a long bridge. I hadn't even seen the bridge, but the fear was still there.

Don't be afraid to cross the bridge that scares you, for it is that very bridge that will take you to new places that you have never been before. Any fear is to be faced. It will be scary at first, but each time that you struggle through the fear, it will get easier and easier.

I can now go over bridges. Some are easier than others, but I always want to see what is on the other side.

> *"All bridges can be crossed, so do
> not give up."* **— Unknown**

> *"Courage is being afraid, but going
> on anyhow."* **— Dan Rather**

# 78

## RICHES

You are very rich and don't even realize it. You are a treasure chest filled with possibilities and potential. At times, we are limited on what we can act on and do. Don't ever let go of your dreams though. Keep working on acquiring them. Some dreams may take a few days or months or even years to achieve.

You are you, and you can't put limitations on that fact. Put your dreams into action. Don't hold yourself back. Others may try to control you by not encouraging you. That is usually because of a problem that they have that they are trying to discourage you. They are trying to hold you back—with them.

Be the best that you can be—FOR YOURSELF. Each of us is a treasure from God.

> *"Until you cross the bridge of insecurities, you can't begin to explore your possibilities."* **— Tim Fargo**

# 79

## THANKFUL

Maybe our lives aren't perfect, but we all have something to be thankful for. We have many blessings, but sometimes they are clouded by bad things.

At this time of year, take a few minutes to reflect on where you are in life and what you have. In the negativity there is always positivity. You are stronger than you think. There is an experience in your past that has made you smarter and wiser. BE THANKFUL. You are here for a reason even if it doesn't seem like it right now.

*"Yesterday is history, tomorrow is a mystery, today is a gift of God, which is why we call it a present."* **— Bill Keane**

# 80

## COUNT YOUR BLESSINGS

I t is so nice to get away, but it is also so nice to come home. We don't always realize what we have until we see so many people who have less. I see many people with many blessings that they take for granted, and I see people just trying to make a dollar to maybe feed their family.

If we have a place to live, and food to eat, and a bed to sleep in at night, we have so many blessings. If we are free to worship as we want to and free to think as we want to, we are so blessed.

Look around today and count your blessings. There is always someone who has more struggles, disadvantages, or heartaches than you do.

> *"Don't think of the thing you didn't get after praying. Think of the countless blessings God gave you without asking."* **— Unknown**

# 81

## Differences

The petals of different flowers are all unique. An onion has many different layers. We are not that much different from flowers and onions. Everyone is different in stature, personality, habits, and traits. Accepting these differences is not always easy. We tend to have our idea of how a person should act and how they should look.

We all need to be more tolerant and accepting of other individuals. We should also welcome the differences in ourselves. We are all different. God designed us that way.

Hopefully, life brings you comfort in your own individuality and more tolerance for others. God Bless You.

> *"Resolve to be tender with the young, compassionate with the aged, sympathetic with the striving and tolerant of the weak and the wrong. At sometime in life you have been all of these."* **— George Washington Carver**

# 82

***

# DISAPPOINTMENTS
# IN LIFE

There are many disappointments in life. I don't know anyone who escapes them. How do we deal with the disappointments? We count all of the positives and blessings that we have.

I just lost a nephew that I thought the world of. But I did get to see the wonderful person that he became, and I enjoyed his accomplishments. He knew no stranger. He was polite and kind to everyone that he came in contact with. He was a wonderful son, sibling, uncle, nephew, and friend. I am a better person for knowing him.

We will all lose someone, sometime in our life. Remember the good things and the good times. What a blessing to be able to think of the positives that someone has brought to our lives.

> *"Live life to the fullest, and focus on the positive."* **— Matt Cameron**

# 83

---

# NEW
# BEGINNINGS

Sunrises are so beautiful. The morning always brings new hope. It is so quiet then, and the sunrise brings new beginnings. We don't know what the day will bring, but we can be hopeful and determined to make it a good day with good experiences.

We tend to think that good experiences always involve other people. But we forget about ourselves. Make it a good day and do something nice for yourself. Read a book, get a massage, spend time just meditating. We all need to pamper ourselves sometimes.

> *"Self care is not selfish. You cannot serve from an empty vessel."* **— Eleanor Brown**

# 84

POSSIBILITIES

What are we psychologically made up of? We don't know. God made you so you can't know until you explore the possibilities. We all have talents and abilities that sometimes go unnoticed and untapped. Try new things. Go on new adventures.

I didn't think about writing until much later in life. My friend suggested it, so I thought I would give it a try. You know what? I really enjoy it and putting words on paper has been so cathartic for me. I even keep a pen and paper by my bed because thoughts have come to me in the night. Many thoughts have been written down in the dark and then I have to decipher them in the morning.

Take the time to discover what God has already blessed you with.

YOU ARE JUST WAITING TO BE FULFILLED.

*"Writing is the best way to talk without being interrupted."* **— Jules Renard**

# 85

## HAPPINESS

Happiness is a state of mind. There are so many feelings attached to happiness. I think that we can all agree that happiness is a much better feeling than sadness. There are times that we have a roller coaster of feelings. It's hard to discern our feelings at times and know what to do, or what the outcome might be.

We can control our own happiness. It might not be easy, but we are in control of our mind. No one else knows what we are thinking. Think only good thoughts and pretty soon you will be believing them.

Happiness is contagious. We all need a smile or good deed to come our way. Just be sure to pay it forward and do the same for someone else.

*"Nobody is in charge of your happiness*
*except you."* **— Anonymous**

*"Happiness is like jam. You can't spread even a little*
*without getting some on yourself."* **— Anonymous**

# 86

## WE ARE
## HUMAN

Have you ever said this to yourself: "I just know that I don't know?" I found myself saying this to myself the other day. There is so much that we are never going to know or remember. (I have a problem remembering details.) Getting upset with the situation just doesn't help. I have tried alphabetizing what I need to remember. I have tried making up a song with the details. I have tried making notes, but that's not always possible. Sometimes, nothing works.

You know, we are not perfect. We are not always going to remember everything. We are not going to know everything. The situation is in the past. Just hold your head up, breathe, and go on. We usually remember the important things in our life, so don't be hard on yourself for forgetting or for not remembering something.

WE ARE HUMAN, NOT PERFECT.

> *"Perfect people aren't real, and real people are not perfect."* **— Unknown**

# 87

## EMOTIONAL WALLS

At times, we face walls in our lives — walls that other people put up to protect themselves, emotionally and physically. Most of us, at one time or another, have put up walls ourselves. We may do this so that we won't be vulnerable to emotional hurts. Does that really stop our chances of being hurt? Usually, the only one to get hurt when we put up walls, is us. We withdraw and don't allow ourselves to get close to a person or situation. We miss out on feeling loved and needed.

Changing these feelings takes baby steps. Little by little we need to trust and allow closeness to occur. It is lonely being behind a wall. Let's break through and be determined to break down the walls that surround us.

There is beauty all around us that we can't see if we are behind a wall. FREE YOURSELF.

> *"The walls we build around us to keep sadness out also keeps out the joy."* — **Jim Rohn**

> *"Instead of a wall, build a window."* — **June Elaine**

# 88

# MOTIVATION

One of the definitions of "motivation" is the desire or willingness to do something; enthusiasm. Motivation can also be determined by our surroundings, weather conditions, feelings, health, or a number of other things. Sometimes not being motivated is Mother Nature telling us to slow down and relax a little.

I thought of this word, motivation, because I am truly not motivated today. The weather is cold and it is dreary out. I don't want to go out and I am not motivated to do much in the house. Maybe it's a good day to read or write.

We shouldn't be upset for feeling this way. We can't always be productive and solve all of the needs of those around us.

The definition of "meditate" is to think deeply or focus one's mind for a period of time in silence. Maybe this is what we can do when we are not motivated.

*"Today is life — the only life you are sure of. Make the most of today. Get interested in something. Shake yourself awake. Develop a hobby. Let the winds of enthusiasm sweep through you. Live today with gusto."* **— Dale Carnegie**

# 89

❦

# CONNECTING
# WITH FRIENDS

Connecting with an old friend is such a blessed event. This just happened to me and it was so nice to be together again. We have known each other for fifty years, but our paths have taken us in different directions. Good and bad has occurred in our lives, but we both seem like the same people that we were back then.

Don't hesitate to call someone from your past. It could be a bright spot in both of your lives. To reminisce and just relax is such a nice distraction from our daily routine.

Make it a point this week to contact someone from your past, or call an old friend to have lunch. You will feel good and they will be overjoyed.

The friends that you have known for some time are the best kind of friends.

> *"Make new friends, but keep the old. One is silver, the other gold."* — **Joseph Parry**

> *"Many people will walk in and out of your life, but only true friends will leave footprints in your heart."* — **Eleanor Roosevelt**

# 90

HEARTBREAKS
AND FEELINGS

You have to care, and love, in order to have a broken heart. If someone doesn't care, do they end up with a broken heart? Of course not. They just go on to the next relationship. Hopefully, at some point, a person finds a true relationship with someone that shares love and caring.

We all hope for the perfect scenario. There are so many people who only think of themselves and what they can gain from a situation. There are those people who never share their feelings because of the fear of having their heart broken. Maybe you have been there.

Sometimes taking a chance on finding out the true feelings of another person has great rewards. With great caution, I did this myself. What a delightful surprise. Even in the autumn of my life, I have found great contentment and love. DON'T GIVE UP. You never know what God has planned for you.

> *"A heartbreak is a blessing from God. It's just His way of letting you realize He saved you from the wrong person."* **— Unknown**

> *"A broken heart loves better than one that has never been hurt."* **— Unknown**

# 91

---

## WHERE DOES
## THE TIME GO?

Where does the time go? Time just flies. It seems like the older one gets, the faster time goes. Do you have goals at the start of a new month? Make a few goals for yourself that you know you can attain and then one or two that you are not sure of, but can work towards. We always need a goal to reach for. Make a "to do" list. If we cross off what we have done, we see our progress and feel good about ourselves.

I hope that I am not the only one who has to make notes and lists to remind myself of what needs to be done. Our lives are too hectic at times to remember appointments, the kid's practice, meals, etc.

Be kind to yourself. We all forget things. We can't be everywhere and do everything. And, by the way, don't forget to schedule time for yourself. WE ARE IMPORTANT. Things wouldn't get done if it weren't for us.

> *"The bad news is time flies. The good news is that you're the pilot."* **— Unknown**

> *"Learn to appreciate what you have before time makes you appreciate what you had."* **— Unknown**

# 92

❧

# DO THEY KNOW
# EVERYTHING?

S ome people may think that they know everything, but if they did, we wouldn't need each other.

The world is full of people who think that they have all of the answers and that they don't need anyone else in their life. There are those people who think that they are perfect at everything. What a sad place this world would be if we didn't need one another, though. Yes, some people can drive us crazy with their "knowledge" and their "stories," but that is when we make our choices as to whom we want to be around.

We most likely have known these types of people. Do we know everything? No, and neither do they. Don't let them get to you and don't argue with them. It's not worth it. We won't change their mind. After all, in their minds they are always right.

> *"A wise man never knows all, only fools know everything."* **— Proverb**

> *"I don't need to know everything. I just need to know where to find it when I need it."* **— Albert Einstein**

# 93

## BEING
## SUCCESSFUL

You have everything that you need to be successful, but you may be lacking the confidence to go after it. We all have thoughts and dreams. We don't always know how to put them into action.

Each day we get a day older. Another day has gone by and we haven't fulfilled our dreams. I know that it is not easy. We are raising kids and making a home for our family. Our time is filled with responsibilities.

Take time to determine what you want to be successful at. Your goal might be a career that you have thought about for some time. It may be going back to school to work towards a degree. Success to you may be becoming the best home-maker that you can be for your family.

Chase after your dream. If you don't, no one else will. YOU CAN DO IT!!!

> *"Work hard in silence, let success*
> *be your voice."* **— Unknown**

> *"Success doesn't come to you. You*
> *go to it."* **— Marva Collins**

# 94

## UPSET

There are times in our lives that we set ourselves up for an upset. Have you ever done something that you knew wouldn't work, and then you got angry at the situation because it didn't work?

Maybe we don't take the time to think through what we are about to do. The world seems to be in such a rush and we find ourselves going at the same fast pace. Some people seem to always be upset with themselves, and with other people. I don't think that they take the time to think, breathe, and analyze what they are about to do.

Life, as we know it, can be upsetting enough. Day-to-day events are a challenge sometimes. Let's not make matters worse for ourselves. LET'S NOT SET OURSELVES UP FOR THAT UPSET.

*"Don't set yourself up for an upset."* — **June Elaine**

# 95

---

## There Is Beauty
## All Around Us

The sun is shining. There is a slight breeze; it is a beautiful day. We don't always stop to see the beauty around us. We take so much for granted.

I have a friend who is legally blind. She can't see the details that most of us can. The leaves and flowers—the color of someone's eyes. Most of all, she can't read her books, drive, or see the computer screen anymore.

We all need to count our blessings each day. There is so much beauty around us that many people can't and never will be able to see. We get so busy, and into such routines, that we forget to think about and see the good in our lives.

Recently, I visited a botanical garden. If you have one near you, take the time to go. The different kinds of trees and beautiful flowers and especially the butterfly garden are amazing! Oh my, so peaceful, calming, and so serene. Enjoy the beauty. Thank you, God, for your gifts.

> *"The only thing worse than being blind, is having sight, but no vision."* **— Helen Keller**

# 96

## BEING
## DIFFERENT

You can't be afraid of being different. There are too many people in the world who try to be like someone else. They feel that it will make them fit in with the crowd.

You are an individual and the only one like you. BE YOU. Some may ridicule you, but guess what? They are most likely jealous. Most people don't know how to handle someone or something that is outside of their thinking. They may put you down or criticize you, but you just keep going, do your own thing, and feel good about yourself.

DON'T BE AFRAID TO BE DIFFERENT. Do things your own way—and own it. Look in the mirror and smile. You are a beautiful person and there is no one else like you.

*"Beauty is about living your life and being happy with yourself, inside and out, and not worrying about what people think of you. You were given this life because you were strong enough to live it."* — **Unknown**

# 97

## COMMITMENT

Have you ever been asked where are you going in life? My answer is, "I will not know where I'm going, until I get there." We all can have goals and plans, and our hope is to fulfill them, but we won't be content until we feel that we have accomplished what we set out to do.

My grandson will be entering college this fall. He has changed his mind on what his major will be several times. The fact is, he has several interests, but he won't know the right one to choose until he has experienced them. He won't know where he is going until he gets there.

Don't hesitate to explore. We all get into a routine, a rut, in our lives. Try something new today. It doesn't have to be something big or a long-term commitment. Do something new for YOU.

*"Without commitment, nothing happens."* **— T.D. Jakes**

# 98

## PARENTING

If you are a parent, you are always a parent, but you don't have to parent forever. As a parent, we always feel the need to be protective, encouraging, and always emotionally there for our children. That will most likely never change, but there comes a time when we need to let go.

It's hard to let go. We have been with them and guided them for so many years. A love has been built in our hearts, because they are a part of us. There comes a time, though, for them to face the real world. We don't have to parent them forever. Our children have to use their own judgement and find their own way of navigating life.

Hopefully, we will always be there to pick them up if they fall. Our children should always know that we will be there for them. Basically, there is an age and a time when they have to begin to "parent themselves." Always put your child in God's hands.

*"Each day of our lives we make deposits in the memory banks of our children."* **— Charles R. Swindoll**

# 99

## HAPPINESS

Happiness comes in all shapes and sizes and in all kinds of events. Some happiness comes from our own doing and choices. We can choose to see a situation as sad or we can determine that there is something good in everything and find happiness. I will admit that this is not always easy. Sometimes we get so bogged down by circumstances that it is hard to see beyond what we are dealing with at the time.

We were dealt this hand. We have got to play it like a pro. Happiness and beauty are all around us, but sometimes we wait for happiness to find us. Don't wait. Go find the happiness in your life.

> *"Happiness is not something you postpone*
> *for the future; it is something you design*
> *for the present."* — **Jim Rohn**

# 100

*❦*

## LOVE GOD,
## YOURSELF,
## AND OTHERS

Put love first. LOVE God, LOVE yourself, and LOVE others. We oftentimes put others before ourselves, but we must love God first. If we don't love ourselves, we also can't effectively love others.

Vow to set aside some time each day as quiet time with yourself. It may be only a few minutes, but relax, breathe, and reflect the best that you can. There are days and times that it is almost impossible to have that time to yourself. We have got to learn and accept that it is crucial to have some quiet alone time. The world and our responsibilities are so demanding these days that we forget about God and ourselves at times.

We have to change these old habits and replace them with new, beneficial ones. You will find the new habits so rewarding. Don't wait until something tragic forces you to change. Put your priorities in order.

> *"Good things happen when you set your priorities straight."* — **Scott Caan**

> *"God's love is like an ocean; you can see its beginning, but not its end."* — **Rick Warren**

# 101

⚜

# BE ALL
# THAT YOU CAN
# BE — BLOOM

I want you TO BE ALL THAT YOU CAN BE. We all have so much potential. Most of it goes untapped, either because of our circumstances, or our insecurities. We have to get up the courage to step out of our box and try to do something for ourselves. We may witness a failure or a "no," but keep on pursuing your dreams.

Most of us have had a "no" in our lives—some of us, many times, but we are still breathing. Keep going and keep pursuing that dream. If YOU don't, no one else will. Take baby steps at first, and before you know it, you will be running toward your dream. YOU CAN DO IT!

If someone would have told me five years ago that I would write a book, I would have laughed in their face. But guess what? I have a book coming out and I am working on another one! WE CAN DO IT, whatever that dream may be.

*"Don't give up on your dreams, or your dreams will give up on you."* — **John Wooden**

# EPILOGUE

This book was written to inspire someone "TO BE ALL THAT THEY CAN BE." Hopefully, each person reading this book will take away a few words of inspiration, and be more willing and able to pursue their dreams.

# EXTRA LOVE

## LOVE

❧

# SETBACKS IN LIFE

We all have setbacks in life. It's how we deal with them that sets us apart. Hopefully we keep forging ahead, and say to ourselves that this setback is not going to get me down or defeat me.

I have just had a physical setback at a busy time in my life. After accepting the fact, I got busy and made calls, canceled appointments, and commitments. None of these are more important than my health. The rest of the people involved will survive quite nicely.

Sometimes our thoughts go to, "I have to do this and I've got to go there," and we think that we must try to accomplish what we have committed to. No commitment or appointment is more important than our well-being.

You can't be helpful to others if you don't take care of yourself first.

*"Things happen so that something worse doesn't happen. God has a plan."*— **June Elaine**

www.ingramcontent.com/pod-product-compliance
Lightning Source LLC
Chambersburg PA
CBHW070925030426
42336CB00014BA/2538